EXPLORING CAREERS IN THE GAMING INDUSTRY

Celia McCarty

San Diego, CA

© 2023 ReferencePoint Press, Inc.
Printed in the United States

For more information, contact:
ReferencePoint Press, Inc.
PO Box 27779
San Diego, CA 92198
www.ReferencePointPress.com

ALL RIGHTS RESERVED.
No part of this work covered by the copyright hereon may be reproduced or used in any form or by any means—graphic, electronic, or mechanical, including photocopying, recording, taping, web distribution, or information storage retrieval systems—without the written permission of the publisher.

LIBRARY OF CONGRESS CATALOGING-IN-PUBLICATION DATA

Names: McCarty, Celia, author.
Title: Exploring careers in the gaming industry / by Celia McCarty.
Description: San Diego, CA : ReferencePoint Press, Inc., 2023. | Includes bibliographical references and index.
Identifiers: LCCN 2022002261 (print) | LCCN 2022002262 (ebook) | ISBN 9781678203344 (library binding) | ISBN 9781678203351 (ebook)
Subjects: LCSH: Video games--Design--Juvenile literature. | Video games industry--Juvenile literature.
Classification: LCC GV1469.3 .M3835 2023 (print) | LCC GV1469.3 (ebook) | DDC 794.8/3--dc23/eng/20220224
LC record available at https://lccn.loc.gov/2022002261
LC ebook record available at https://lccn.loc.gov/2022002262

CONTENTS

Introduction: Working in the Business of Play	4
Game Artist	7
Game Designer	15
Game Programmer	22
Pro Gamer	30
Sound Designer	38
Game Tester	46
Source Notes	53
Interview with a Game Designer	56
Other Jobs in the Gaming Industry	59
Index	60
Picture Credits	63
About the Author	64

INTRODUCTION: WORKING IN THE BUSINESS OF PLAY

For someone whose passion is gaming, the idea of earning a living playing video games sounds like a dream come true. In this exciting industry, game makers and professional gamers share common traits: they have a passion for gaming, they are highly skilled, and they work well with others.

Making a video game is typically a group effort. Creating a successful big-budget game means that hundreds of workers, artists, programmers, testers, and designers are brought together to work toward the same goal. With so many creative people working in specific areas of game design, it can be challenging to keep everyone on the same page. Senior narrative director Mary DeMarle describes how she and her writing team developed the characters for Marvel's *Guardians of the Galaxy* video game:

> Every Friday we would have script reads for like two hours. . . . And we acted out the characters ourselves as we're doing it. . . .
>
> And I think by doing it every Friday it kind of got everyone laughing and joking and talking about these characters and basically embracing them for who they are. And that kind of helped a lot for maintaining a consistency across all of the scripts. . . . It ended up being a lot of fun.[1]

The fun and creativity of making games with coworkers who share that passion is one of the benefits of working in the game industry. But making games is only part of the industry. Professional gamers are another part. They play competitive games on esports teams, putting in countless hours of practice together to help win competitions. The fun and camaraderie of playing and competing at a very high skill level with others who love gaming are part of what attracts these athletes to play games for a living.

Pro gamer Joseph "Luzuh" Loose's esports team Rix.GG enjoys the excitement and energy of playing together in person. For some time, Rix.GG was unable to practice in person at "bootcamp" due to the COVID-19 pandemic. When the members were finally able to meet and practice together just before Riot Games' *Valorant* Champions Tour qualifiers, Loose was ecstatic. "The best thing about bootcamp for me was being next to everyone in a line," enthused Loose. "It felt great playing these really super important games that we would normally play online together. Just seeing everybody physically in person getting hyped . . . fist bumping and screaming, and just hyping each other up to another level."[2]

Game Industry Challenges

Making games can be a massive undertaking, and many game makers resort to excessive overtime, or "crunch," in an attempt to complete games more quickly. A 2021 survey by the International Game Developers Association (IGDA) revealed that about 60 percent of game workers crunched, or worked long hours. Crunch can cause mental and physical health issues and lead to burnout.

Job insecurity is another issue facing people in the game industry. A studio may lay off game makers when it completes a game, for example, or professional gamers can be cut from an esports team at any time. According to the 2021 IGDA survey, employed and self-employed workers average more than 2 jobs in a five-year period. Freelancers and contractors have 4.3 jobs in five years, on average.

Gender discrimination and harassment also occur at some companies. Activision Blizzard and Riot Games settled discrimination lawsuits for $18 million in 2022 and $100 million in 2021.

Commenting on the lawsuits, 2021 Game Awards producer Geoff Keighley tweeted, "There is no place for abuse, harassment or predatory practices in any company or any community."[3] As in other industries, it is hoped that legal actions may help change game industry culture. In December 2021 Vodeo Games became the first game studio in North America to form a union, and in January 2022 quality assurance testers at Raven Software formed Activision Blizzard's first union, requesting the company recognize the union. Giving workers the means to speak out against long hours, discrimination, and other problems in the workplace will help many pursue their talents in a safe and productive environment.

A Rewarding Career

Despite these issues, many designers, programmers, artists, and players thrive in a creative industry they love. Amalie Kae shares, "Writing for a video game is one of the most satisfying things I have ever done creatively."[4] For those like Kae who want to be involved in making the kinds of games they enjoy playing, or like Loose who are interested in playing competitively, a game industry career can be extremely rewarding.

GAME ARTIST

What Does a Game Artist Do?

Artists in the video game industry create settings and characters and tell stories that engage players. Their work evokes feelings and emotions that help immerse players in the game.

It all starts with concept artists collaborating with designers to determine the game's appearance. For example, if the game takes place in ancient Greece or medieval Europe, the concept artists set appropriate historical themes and tones that the other artists will follow. Once the concept is established, other artists take over. For instance, character artists define each game character through qualities like color, posture, stance, musculature, and clothing. User interface artists design graphical menus showing important gameplay information such as player stats or game time remaining.

While a simple game may have only one or a few artists performing several of these roles, a large studio has many specialized artists. Environment artists build the game world except for the characters, including landscape, sky, buildings, rooms, and items in a room. Technical artists are hybrid artist-programmers who use software, for example,

A Few Facts

Number of Jobs
About 60,000 in 2020

Pay
Median annual salary of $64,725

Educational Requirements
Bachelor's degree

Personal Qualities
Creative, artistic, good communicator

Work Settings
Office or remote

Future Job Outlook
Growth of 16 percent through 2030

to build skeletons that help characters move naturally. Character animators then use movement and poses to portray personality and perform gameplay actions. Visual effects artists add excitement by rendering weather and environmental effects, explosions, magical powers, motion blurs, and other gameplay features.

A Typical Workday

A game artist alternates between teamwork and solo work on highly creative projects. The day often starts with team updates and collaboration on projects. A project might be animating a character's hand or recording a character's script for a scene. Artists draw, paint, act, sculpt, play instruments, and also use software tools. Visual effects artist Steve Kaplan describes a project: "I needed to write code, to understand physics, to work through the technicalities of animating a thing. . . . Sometimes I needed to hand-animate how wind would react with a cloth instead of being able to use a physics engine [software program]."[5] Deciding what tool will best accomplish the given task is part of the expertise of game artists.

Whether an artist works in a studio or remotely, collaboration is a big part of the job. Senior concept artist Allie Strom reveals, "That moment where you're with your team with all these drawings and taking them through like all the things that excited you and got you like super ramped up to make these drawings in the first place, and connecting those things to those ideas that took you down that journey. That's really where the magic is."[6]

Working alone or with a team, the artist spends a typical day designing, drawing, animating, or otherwise enhancing elements of a game so that players will have a positive, immersive experience when the project is completed.

Education and Training

Most employers prefer a game artist to have at least a bachelor's degree in a related field like art or computer science. In addition, experience playing or making a variety of games can assist game

> ## Having Fun on the Job
>
> "I started off doing character animation, but because I also had a general background in 3D art . . . my supervisors approached me about doing effects full-time. I honestly had never considered that path because . . . frankly, it seemed too fun to be a real career! . . . My favorite part of this job is the 'wow' factor. In large part, special effects exist to make the player think: 'Oh, wow, look at that!' . . . Delivering that kind of visually impressive moment holds tremendous appeal for me, particularly when I'm tackling something I've never made before."
>
> —Nathaniel Hubbell, special effects artist
>
> Quoted in James W. Bay, "How to Become a Video Game Special Effects Artist," Game Industry Career Guide, September 7, 2021. www.gameindustrycareerguide.com.

artists in understanding the ways their art will contribute to the games they are designing.

Becoming a game artist requires a great deal of preparation. Artists master their craft and develop their unique style with daily practice, such as drawing, painting, sculpting, and modeling. To make characters and environments feel natural, artists must be great observers of the world around them. Gino Whitehall, a senior visual concept artist, recommends, "Have your sketchbook everywhere you go. Pull it out anytime you're waiting for food, anytime you're standing in line. Have it as a natural extension of your body. You can really learn a lot simply from observation."[7]

Putting all this practice and preparation to use in creating a portfolio or demonstration reel is good training. Prospective employers want to see polished samples of an applicant's best work.

Skills and Personality

Artists are very skilled craftspeople who also use software tools and may code. Visual artists' traditional skills—such as drawing,

Game artists share ideas about artwork that will be incorporated into a video game. At some stages, artists work alone. At other stages, they collaborate with team members to transform initial concepts into animated characters.

modeling, composition, photography, and anatomy—underpin solid software skills. Artists need to have technical skills, such as fluency with Adobe Creative Cloud. Artists who are also proficient with game engines, animation, and other software are in high demand. Concept artist Tyler Finney says, "Insist on developing a range of skills that make you a multi-threat. . . . Often when selecting applicants to fill a role, we chose the artist that has decent paint skills but also knows Maya/3DS Max and After Effects over the artist that is clearly a better painter yet lacks other software proficiency. The more things you are interested in and skilled at, the more valuable you are to the employer."[8]

As for personality, game artists must be good communicators, team players, and especially problem solvers. Many game designers like to create unique worlds that feel different from others on the market, so artists should enjoy imagining new environments, interesting soundscapes, and strange characters. As special effects artist Nathaniel Hubbell explains, "Very often you'll be assigned something you've never done before. Who knows—

a waterfall that flows up? An exploding star? A cloak made of starlight? A dust storm that's alive? If you enjoy tackling weird, unpredictable challenges, this is an exciting area to be in."[9]

Game artists are also continually acquiring new skills and should enjoy the challenge of learning on or off the job. Senior character artist Willem van der Schyf offers encouragement: "If it's not hard, you're not learning. So don't be afraid of struggling a little bit."[10]

Working Conditions

About half of video game artists work for studios in an office. Some work remotely but adhere to a typical workday schedule. Self-employed artists often manage their own schedule. Rich Werner, a 2-D artist/animator, for example, sets his own hours. "Since I work for myself these days," he says, "I usually get up and drink coffee, take the kids to school then come home and start drawing or animating. I have my daily conference call and then I get back into 'work mode' by 10:30 a.m. When the kids get home, I take a break until they go to bed and then get back to work again until around midnight or 2 a.m."[11]

Even remote workers come into the office at times or collaborate online. Making games with talented teammates is a big perk. Sometimes, the game designers get to work with famous actors, composers, choreographers, and stunt coordinators who lend their talents to the game world. Animation director Gabriel Rountree worked on the video games related to *The Matrix* films. He shares an experience from working on one of the games, which utilized his favorite Chinese film director, Yuen Woo-ping:

> I grabbed all of Yuen Woo-ping's movies and found stuff that felt like it fit *The Matrix*.
>
> The stunt team was insane. They would go through and do the most incredible work, they would do it all day. . . . It was absolutely incredible. The only time I was star struck during the whole thing was when I met Yuen Woo-ping.[12]

What It Takes to Succeed as an Artist or Animator in Video Games

"You have to LOVE art for sure. You have to have that passion to create. If you want to create art for games, or any art-related job—It has to be in your blood. Draw SOMETHING every day! Even if it is just some quick doodles on a napkin. You also have to be pretty easy-going. Being able to take an idea—no matter how long and hard you've worked on it—and then be willing to toss it out and start over if necessary. That can happen a bunch. You have to be able to let it go and keep moving forward."

—Rich Werner, 2-D artist and animator

Quoted in James W. Bay, "Meet Rich Werner, 2D Artist/Animator Behind 'Plants vs Zombies,'" Game Industry Career Guide, July 18, 2020. www.gameindustrycareerguide.com.

There are hazards. Crunch is common at some companies. It can lead to physical and mental health concerns. Head, neck, wrist, and hand injuries can occur from overwork and repetitive movements. For some, repeated exposure to violence in video games can damage mental health.

Employers and Pay

As films incorporate more animation and special effects and video games become more cinematic, artists increasingly cross over between motion picture and game studios. It is not uncommon for visual artists to take jobs from both worlds, especially if these individuals work for themselves.

According to Salary.com, the average salary for special effects artists and animators in 2020 was $64,725 a year. However, there are many types of artists and a large range of pay for each specific artistic field. Some employers pay a bonus if the company is enjoying financial success. Despite pervasive crunch, most game artists do not receive additional pay for working overtime because they are either a salaried employee or a contractor paid a set amount.

What Is the Future Outlook for Game Artists?

The game industry is fast growing with increasing demand for game content. As technology improves, gamers expect more realistic animation, real-time effects, and cinematic quality. These features are very labor intensive and require more artists to create them. The Bureau of Labor Statistics estimates faster-than-average growth for fine artists (14 percent) and for special effects/animators (16 percent) through 2030. Even though the growth percentages are healthy, the number of people in the industry is relatively small, and there is a lot of competition. Game artists are also subject to unstable employment. Some artists start by having a full-time job and do art gigs on the side to gain experience. Once they build their portfolios, they may be able to get a full-time job in the industry.

Find Out More

Academy of Interactive Arts & Sciences Foundation (AIAS)
www.aiasfoundation.org
The AIAS awards scholarships to students (and professionals early in their career), including the AIAS Foundation Scholarship and the WomenIn Scholarship. Those interested in a video game career can apply to the AIAS mentoring program and Amplifying New Voices workshop for training and coaching from industry professionals.

Real-Time VFX
https://realtimevfx.com
This website offers information and inspiration for special effects artists. Artists share their sketchbooks here, and there is a forum

for those just getting started. The site also has a question-and-answer section, tools, tutorials, and a weekly stream.

***So You Wanna Make Games??*, Riot Games**
www.youtube.com/watch?v=RqRoXLLwJ8g
Riot Games presents this excellent series of videos featuring different types of game artists explaining aspects of what they do and how they do it.

GAME DESIGNER

What Does a Game Designer Do?

Game designers envision and oversee the creation of video games. Designers bring together enticing, fun, and challenging gameplay with an interesting game story filled with intriguing plots and captivating characters. While one person can design a simple game, on more complex projects, teams of designers, artists, and programmers work together to bring a game concept to life.

On big-budget games, senior-level designers with titles like *lead designer* or *creative director* oversee the entire game development. These designers start with an idea for a game and then attempt to persuade game studio management to invest in creating it. If the studio accepts the project, the lead designer guides the game team in creating it.

Other types of designers follow the direction of the lead designer. Content designers develop the game concept and layout. Game mechanics designers plan gameplay—the rules, the obstacles, the rewards, and the levels of victory. Designers who contribute to the writing of the game have

A Few Facts

Number of Jobs
About 156,000 in 2020

Pay
Median annual salary of $70,471

Educational Requirements
Bachelor's degree

Personal Qualities
Passion for gaming, creative, good communicator, problem solver

Work Settings
Office or remote

Future Job Outlook
Growth of about 2 percent per year through 2024

titles such as game writers, story editors, or narrative designers. It is these designers who write an engaging story and who describe the characters in depth to guide the work of the game artists. They also write any character dialogue.

A Typical Workday

A video game designer's day is a mix of individual and group creative work. New designers often start as level designers. A level designer sketches concepts and uses game design software to create a layout for one level of a game. Level designers work closely with artists and programmers in creating the elements of the level, such as gameplay mechanics, setting, and obstacles.

Collaboration is key in the creative process. Creative director Richard Lambert describes how teams collaborate in person. "When you're all in the office at the same time," he says, "it's really easy to walk by somebody's desk and go, 'Hey, that doesn't quite look right. What are you working on?' Or somebody can go, 'Hey, I have this really brilliant idea.' . . . And they talk it through right then and there." But Lambert notes that as many positions switch to remote work, the collaboration faces obstacles. "With everybody working from home," he says, "you have to message them, 'Hey, are you there?' 'Hey, can we have 10 minutes to talk on Teams or on a Skype call?'"[13] Remote work is becoming more common—especially in light of the COVID-19 pandemic—and game companies are adjusting to design meetings that require virtual attendance.

As a team works to create a game, designers evaluate whether the elements are working as designed and whether the gameplay is fun. All games go through ongoing testing to find and fix bugs, or programming errors. And at the end of the workday, members of the game team gather for a playthrough of the parts of the game they have been working on to assess their progress.

The creativity, collaboration, and challenges of a designer's work ensure variety in each day. Designer Pete Low shares, "In

A Very Cool Job That Is Not for Everyone

"Game design is a very cool job if you like to collaborate, communicate with people, think about games at a mechanical level, and are willing to take harsh feedback at times. However, it is not a career for everyone. You will need to have thick skin and lots of confidence to keep going even after people destroy your features or ideas when testing them. . . . If it is what you want, and you have the skills . . . I think being a game designer is great because you never get bored . . . and most importantly it is super fun."

—Chris Muriel, game level designer

Chris Muriel, *What Does a Game Designer Do on a Daily Basis in the AAA Industry?*, Game Design with Chris, YouTube, August 31, 2020. www.youtube.com/watch?v=FjcP9OJRfEE.

over 17 years of working in the video game industry I can't say that I've had a typical working day, which I'm sure is why I still love the job."[14]

Education and Training

While degrees in computer science and game design are very helpful to those interested in a career in the field, degrees in other disciplines—such as the fine arts, sciences, and liberal arts—can also prepare designers. High school and college courses in subjects such as statistics, art, architecture, physics, computer science, and history are a good foundation for game design.

Employers may require a college degree, but some hire video game designers based on their portfolio or demo reel and their experience. Creating a polished portfolio or demo reel of high-quality work is good training to be a game designer. Aspiring designers also gain important knowledge by playing many types of games, making and "modding" (modifying) games, and immersing themselves in popular culture through films and books. An internship or any game industry job, such as game testing, is another way to gain valuable work experience.

Skills and Personality

A deep interest in gaming is what fuels designers, and acquiring writing, game engine, and coding skills allows designers to put that interest to work. A lead designer who goes by the name MeaningfulChoices suggests that an aspiring designer should

> be really good at something specific. You want a solid foundation in all the design basics, but you want to excel at some area. Have your portfolio show off that expertise. If you're great at making multiplayer FPS [first-person shooter] maps, I want to see that map. I want to see your design process for why you built it that way, a top down view, a (quick) video going through it. Even if I'm not making a multiplayer FPS, I might be impressed by it enough to start a conversation.[15]

Designers work well with others. They convey their ideas clearly, listen carefully, and respect others' opinions. PlayStation level designer Chris Muriel says:

> A big part of a designer job is communication. You work alongside very talented people who think differently, like artists and programmers. Because they have different perspectives and abilities, you need to be clear when you ask something from them. The last thing you want is to waste their time because your communication was unclear. There is a lot of collaboration between different departments in order to get a feature from concept to completion.[16]

Collaboration includes criticism. Being able to gracefully accept negative feedback helps a designer rethink an idea and adapt to changes.

Working Conditions

If employed by a company, designers may work in an office or remotely. Self-employed designers typically work at home. Generally, game designers work at least forty hours a week, and overtime is common.

Some people who want to be game designers mistakenly believe that creating games is similar to the fun of playing them, but being a designer is hard work. Having one's work criticized or cut from a game, meeting deadlines, and working excessive overtime can be stressful. Designer David Fried says, "One night I was working on a campaign level to the point where I ended up crashing on the sofa at the office. . . . And I woke up the next day . . . a Saturday mind you . . . and continued working. I went home at 6 p.m. to take a shower and sleep in my own bed, and I got reprimanded the next day for not staying for a play through."[17]

Some companies are addressing work-life balance. Lydia Winters, chief storyteller at Mojang Studios, creators of *Minecraft*, says, "We can support teams when they're worried about missing deadlines. . . . [We're] also making sure we really prioritize wellness and being careful that people aren't overworking."[18]

Employment in the game industry is volatile. For instance, an employer may hire hundreds to work on a game during development and then lay them off once the game has been released. In some cases, a designer may be asked to shift into a different role, such as testing or programming. Designer Tom Sloper explains, "Most people who become designers do so through having been either a programmer, tester, customer support . . . or other useful job in a game company. . . . And most game companies cannot sustain full-time positions for 'designers' so it is likely that someone who designs a game will have to fall back on his/her other job duties when that project is over."[19]

Employers and Pay

Game designers generally find jobs with either independent (indie) or large (AAA) studios. Pay ranges are wide due to the varied

Pulling Together a Game's Story

"A game is a machine with a lot of moving parts, and those parts keep changing—and affecting other parts. That means if a level gets cut, the story may have to change. If a mechanic changes, could be time for a rewrite. . . .

At first, writers are surprised that so many other departments can weigh in on the game's story. . . . Game writers learn to chase down the animators, musicians, environment artists, and level designers in the studio, so that together, they can find ways to tell their stories as only games can."

—Susan O'Connor, writer and narrative designer

Susan O'Connor, "Game Writing: Expectations v Reality," Susan O'Connor Writing Studio, January 12, 2022. www.susanoconnorwriter.com.

---

responsibility and experience among designers. Salary.com lists the median pay at over $70,000 per year. GameDesigning.org's 2021 average yearly salary for a designer with zero experience was about $60,000. Other job-reporting websites indicate that in-demand lead designers can make six-figure salaries.

Some designers work solo or with others to create simple games. Josh Wardle, a software engineer, created Wordle, a browser game, for his partner, who loves word games. Wardle put Wordle online in mid-October 2021, and by December 2021 it had gone viral. As of January 2022, there were more than 2 million daily players. Faced with overwhelming demand and mounting server costs, Wardle sold Wordle for an undisclosed seven-figure sum in January 2021.

What Is the Future Outlook for Game Designers?

Recruiter.com estimates about 2 percent growth per year through 2024 for video game designers. Some predict that because of a huge demand for more gaming content, the growth might be higher. Games are increasingly complex, playable for hours on end, and available online around the clock, with new content dropping regularly. Studios need designers to create and update these games. However, there is stiff competition for game designer positions. Aspiring designers must hone their skills, study, and gain experience in order to work in this role.

Find Out More

Academy of Interactive Arts & Sciences (AIAS)
www.interactive.org

This global organization is for those in interactive entertainment industries. Its site features podcasts with game makers, news and press releases, and conversational interviews with industry leaders. Membership is required to take advantage of all the site has to offer.

AIGA
www.aiga.org

Formerly the American Institute of Graphic Arts, AIGA is a membership organization for designers that offers many free resources, including a guide to internships; a free, high school–level basic graphic design curriculum; design articles on topics such as building a portfolio; the *Eye on Design* blog; and access to *Dialectic*, a scholarly journal.

International Game Developers Association (IGDA)
www.igda.org

The IGDA is a nonprofit organization for people who create games. IGDA offers a Discord channel and some programs for students, including: IGDA Scholars awards, discounted student membership, the student portfolio showcase, the student game showcase, and discounts on conferences and game development software.

GAME PROGRAMMER

What Does a Game Programmer Do?

Game programmers turn the vision of designers and artists into reality. Through programming, they transform story and drawing concepts, mere marks on sheets of paper, into exciting, animated characters. They write programs telling computers how to assemble gameplay rules, images, sound, and motion into a playable game. Game programmers implement all the elements of a game, including score keeping and player progress, within a reliable framework. They also build that framework and modify existing software tools for the game.

While one person can program a simple game, on more complex games, programmers specialize in different areas. Game programmers may have titles such as tools programmers, software engineers, or software developers.

Game programmers are creative problem solvers. All sorts of problems arise when making a game. A challenge might be modifying game software to allow characters to fly. For a game with characters moving in zero gravity, game developer Alexander Perrin says he used software

A Few Facts

Pay
Median annual salary of $67,000

Educational Requirements
Bachelor's degree

Personal Qualities
Good communication and problem-solving skills

Work Settings
Office or remote

Future Job Outlook
Growth of 16 percent through 2030*

*Includes software developers in the motion picture and video game industries

called a physics engine to create a "movement system which, with Newtonian mode enabled, allows you to move about the environment with a net force addition of zero. In other words, every action has an equal and opposite reaction!"[20] By building this system, Perrin made it easier for artists, animators, and designers to create natural zero-gravity movement for characters in the game.

As Perrin's team effort to create the illusion of zero gravity shows, making a game is a collaboration. Brian Gish, a game tools programmer, creates applications to make the game team's work easier. He shares, "My favorite part of being a tools programmer is that my customers are the people I work with, so I get instant feedback. . . . When I finish a task people stop by my desk to say thanks and sometimes even buy me cupcakes!"[21]

When a game team requests features, programmers implement and test them. Software development engineers in test (SDETs) are programmers who oversee the work of quality assurance testers. They guide testers on what type of bugs to look for. Generally, when testers find bugs, SDETs fix them. SDETs also write programs instructing computers to check for certain bugs. This saves human testers from some of the more mind-numbing testing.

On an ongoing basis, programmers build and maintain the software systems that team members use to create and deploy games. And, with many games playable online twenty-four hours a day, programmers continue to create game patches that fix errors and add features after a game is launched. For example, speedrunners (players who try to complete a game as fast as possible) exploited a bug in Insomniac Games' *Ratchet & Clank: Rift Apart* that enabled them to skip a lot of the game and finish it in less than two hours. The bug, however, caused most casual players who happened upon it to die in the game. The game team consulted players via chats and Discord events and then created a patch that satisfied everyone. Senior gameplay programmer Matt Graczyk turned the bug into a playable feature that allowed speedrunners to continue to move quickly while not stopping the progress of regular players. "We didn't want a

Programming the Servers That Manage Online Play

"It is actually really fun, and most other engineers view you as a super hero. Most engineers in games focus on gameplay, graphics . . . they want to work on the things that everyone can see. But . . . there is more that goes into creating games. Someone has to write the tech that can process the thousands of analytics events per second that come from game clients, ensure that saved games in the cloud never get lost. . . . Since most engineers don't have a high level of expertise in networking and server development, they soon realize that you are a critical part of the team."

—Elvir Bahtijaragic, game server engineer

Quoted in Jason W. Bay, "How to Become a Video Game Server Engineer," Game Industry Career Guide, 2021. www.gameindustrycareerguide.com.

player to accidentally use it and have their play through ruined, but we also didn't want to rain on the parade of speedrunners, so we made it slightly more complicated to pull off,"[22] explained *Rift Apart*'s game designer.

A Typical Workday

Most workdays, a game development team gathers early for an in-person or online meeting. Programmers provide updates on their progress and assist team members in working out problems. When programmers build a new version of the game, they tell the game team to be sure to enter their work in the latest version.

Back at their desks, programmers catch up on emails, plan their day, and then work on projects. Game developer Shawn Warnock describes a typical project, the creation of a tool to make testing easier. "[It is] software that can interact with your game or application without anyone actually physically interacting with the game," he explains. "It can click buttons, check data, and make verifications. . . . That allows us to find big, high-priority issues faster than a manual testing team usually can."[23] Such projects can cut down the human hours needed to finish a game. Still, programmers often require many months of coding time to piece large games together. A team of programmers might work two or more years to bring a big-budget game to life.

After lunch programmers continue work on projects. They also meet with coworkers, helping artists and designers put their work in the game engine, for example.

Some companies allow time for mentoring. Warnock says, "I have mentors who have been gameplay programmers for a while. I have one-on-ones with some of the higher-level software engineers and with technical directors. They're currently working with me to give me insight and help me grow my skill set—doing exercises and giving me homework to work on. It's almost like getting an internship on top of doing my normal work."[24]

Late in the day the game team gathers for a playthrough. The team plays the part of the game worked on that day to see what does and does not work. The next day, the programmers will tackle the issues that need to be addressed.

Education and Training

Employers often desire programmers to hold a bachelor's degree in disciplines such as software engineering, software development, computer science, or video game design or development. A master's degree is becoming more common among game programmers, though.

Sometimes an employer will hire a software engineering technician, such as a coder, with an associate's degree, especially if the person has experience. Warnock started as a game tester, studying Java and automation tools in his free time. To get a job using his new skills, Warnock left the game industry. He says, "Then, after I got the professional experience, I applied to jobs within the game industry for core automation. It was definitely a lot of work and a lot of dedication to improving [my] art form."[25]

High school preparation includes computer, math, and science courses for technical and analytical skills, and English and speech classes for communication skills. Experience coding, playing, and making games helps a résumé stand out to an employer. Applicants with such experience who also create a polished video of a game to showcase, boost their chances of landing a job.

Skills and Personality

Game programmers need to know programming languages, such as C++, C#, and Java. Employers look for proficiency with game engines like Unity or Unreal. With the trend toward mobile gaming, knowledge of iOS and Android programming is useful.

Video game programmers turn the vision of designers and artists into reality. They write the programs that tell computers how to assemble gameplay rules, images, sound, and motion into a playable game.

The Importance of Tools Programmers

"Most people don't understand that a tools programmer position is needed. It's hard telling people that I work at a game company but nothing I do actually makes it into the final product. I end up explaining that we have a game engine that takes in a ton of raw data and puts the game up on the screen. Then we have artists and designers who are expected to input that raw data. I'm the middle man that makes their lives easier so they can be more efficient and thus more creative."

—Brian Gish, game tools programmer

Quoted in Jason W. Bay, "How to Become a Video Game Tools Programmer," Game Industry Career Guide, 2021. www.gameindustrycareerguide.com.

Game programmers' curiosity, analytical skills, and creativity fuel their problem-solving ability, a core part of the job. Communication skills enable them to fully understand the problem the game team asks them to solve and to clearly present their recommendations, ideas, and solutions to coworkers.

Working Conditions

Most programmers work for a game studio in an office where teams can gather. Generally, people working in the game industry share a love of games, so the office atmosphere can be fun and supportive.

Creating big-budget games, as well as less complex ones, requires many hours of coding and other work activities, often over a period of years. Some studios institute a "crunch culture" of excessive overtime in an attempt to move development more quickly without hiring additional staff. Crunch takes a toll. The long hours can affect physical and mental health, including wrist, hand, neck, back, shoulder, and other injuries. In addition, the work is cyclical; when a game is finished, workers may lose their jobs. And there is a lot of churn—job instability—as projects end or studios close, merge, or lose funding. Many employers reject crunch and provide more stability so that they do not lose good employees. However, it pays to research this aspect of potential employers.

Employers and Pay

According to the Bureau of Labor Statistics (BLS), the median wage for software developers was about $67,000 per year in 2020. Entry-level coders will earn less than the median wage, and those with more experience and responsibility will earn more. The lowest-paid 10 percent earned less than $65,210, and the highest-paid 10 percent earned more than $170,100.

Other factors affecting pay are the size of the employer, whether the programmer has a bachelor's or graduate degree, and the job location. Some employers pay an annual bonus when a company performs well financially, and this can boost pay.

Programmers also work as freelancers or contractors, or they might create games on their own or in small groups. Game maker Markus "Notch" Persson began programming at age seven and created his first game at age eight. He created the popular building game *Minecraft* by himself. Few self-designed games attract as many players as *Minecraft* has, but many programmers make their own games for fun and learn a lot along the way.

What Is the Future Outlook for Game Programmers?

Not only are software developers one of the fastest-growing occupations, they are also among the most highly paid. The BLS estimates that demand for software developers in the motion picture and video game industries will grow by 16 percent through 2030, and some of this growth will be for game programmers. Currently, mobile gaming is a fast-growing area, and as games increasingly implement artificial intelligence and virtual and augmented reality, programmers with these skills will be in particular demand.

Find Out More

Develteam
www.develteam.com
Develteam is a website offering independent game development forums, tools, job boards, and spaces for work samples. Some jobs offered are unpaid.

Game Developer
www.gamedeveloper.com
The Game Developer site contains game industry news, interviews, and articles. For those pursuing a career, there are a career guide, blogs, and job postings.

GameDev.net
https://gamedev.net
This site for people who are developing games offers tutorials on game development, discussion forums, and expert blogs. It also provides spaces for members to display portfolios and projects.

International Game Developers Association (IGDA)
https://igda.org
This global nonprofit group serves the game developer community. Students can vie for IGDA Foundation scholarships or participate in IGDA Scholars coaching, the student portfolio showcase, and the student game showcase. There is a student membership that includes discounts on conferences and game development software.

PRO GAMER

What Does a Pro Gamer Do?

Most professional gamers have loved playing video games since childhood and are uniquely skilled at winning. Pro gamers travel worldwide to compete in tournaments. The tournament is the esports athlete's opportunity to show the results of hard work, whether solo or as a member of a team. Pro gamers practice remotely online and in person in esports team training sites. Practice consists of playing fifty or more hours of popular, competitive video games each week.

As with other professional sports, only the top players win a spot on an esports team. With plenty of talented competition, pro gamers must perform consistently at a high level to stay on the team. Even the best players can be cut from a team if they are in a slump or if team management wants a different player. Most players end up playing on many teams in their short careers. The average esports career ends at age twenty-five. The combination of unstable employment and a short career leads many

A Few Facts

Number of Jobs
About 2,000 globally

Pay
Average annual salary of $48,000

Educational Requirements
None

Personal Qualities
Exceptional game-playing skills, fast reaction times, mental toughness

Work Settings
Online at home or at an esports gaming house or training facility

Global Esports Growth
Projected industry growth of 24 percent in 2023

pro gamers to leverage their celebrity to bring in more stable income.

Esports athletes can supplement their team salary and tournament winnings by streaming gameplay and by promoting companies' products. They may wear branded clothing, drink certain beverages, or advertise gaming equipment in exchange for payment. Streaming platforms, such as Twitch and YouTube, also pay pro gamers for each advertisement shown on their streams. The biggest income boost comes from fans supporting pro gamers by donating and subscribing to their streams. In 2021, followers of Twitch, an online community for streamers, reported that Ali "Myth" Kabbani, a member of Team SoloMid, with more than five thousand subscribers and 7 million followers, earns more than $10 million from Twitch annually. Most pro gamers earn far less, though. To attract and keep followers, streamers entertain, inform, and professionally interact with fans via chat, often while gaming.

A Typical Workday

Esports teams often live together in a team game house, where they can practice together in the same way they will have to perform during tournaments. On the outside, the team house may look like a normal home, but along with living spaces are gaming rooms with state-of-the-art setups and streaming pods.

Perhaps ten team members share the home, eating together, relaxing together, and playing together. The players often maintain a schedule set by the team manager. They wake up, eat breakfast, and exercise with a trainer until noon. Specialists such as chefs, nutritionists, and sports psychologists make sure the players are in good health. As Canadian pro gamer Keagen "P3NGU1N" Smith explains, "They're making sure you're staying healthy and at your peak, because there's a lot of pressure to perform."[26]

After lunch, analysts and coaches lead a strategy session. Team members view video of other teams and go over their own clips to learn new ways of handling gameplay situations. Then the team scrimmages for six hours before breaking for a chef-prepared dinner.

Teams practice a lot, sometimes in friendly games played against teams in other countries. In North America pro gamers often continue to play into the early morning hours and stream at the same time so that they can interact with international audiences too. This can be a dream lifestyle for many players, but training is rigorous, and team members are expected to perform at their best or potentially lose their spot on the team.

Education and Training

No formal education is required to be a pro gamer. Aspiring pro gamers train by playing games and learning from other gamers' streams. They enter esports tournaments that are open to amateur players. While top pro gamers are recruited young, some gamers join their high school and college esports teams where they can train while completing their education.

Prospective pro gamers must learn how to play long hours while also maintaining top physical and mental health. With grueling schedules and intense competition, esports can burn players out. Esports teams are finding that supporting players' health and providing work-life balance leads to success. Better teams provide coaches and sports psychologists to help pro gamers manage issues like anxiety. Exercise also helps with stress. Pro gamers train like any other athletes. Fitness gives a gamer more endurance, speed, flexibility, and focus. Pro gamer Cody Sun says that many teams have rethought the grueling practice schedule that can lead to injuries and burnout. He explains, "It's really hard for us to only have six hours of sleep and practice constantly. I feel like our current approach, or at least the direction of our approach, is making sure we have a healthy lifestyle, and healthy mindset, and then just be really efficient with the practice."[27]

Enjoy the Journey

"If you want to get into gaming seriously, it shouldn't be a desperate quest to become the very best. It should be an enjoyable journey. You can chase success when you get to a certain point. But first, just find out what you enjoy and take it from there. Look at the intricacies of the game you want to get good at. Look at the players who are winning, the players that are losing, and make sense of what they're doing. Join forums, become a part of the community. Ask questions and learn that way. For the most part, just have fun."

—Ryan "Prodigal Son" Hart, British pro gamer

Quoted in Tom Fordy, "Ryan Hart Tells Us Everything About His Life as a Pro Gamer: 'It Sounds Fun, but Gaming Is Definitely Work,'" Askmen India. https://in.askmen.com.

Skills and Personality

Exceptional gameplay skill is the basic requirement to be a pro gamer. Pro gamers must win competitions. With physical and mental attributes similar to Olympic athletes, pro gamers have nearly unmatched hand-eye coordination and fast reflexes. Gamers need mental toughness, including discipline, mental stamina, and the ability to cope with stress. The most successful pro gamers do more than win; they work well with teammates, coaches, and managers. This requires strong communication and leadership skills. Pro gamers often are role models. They play fair and conduct themselves professionally during public events, such as fan meet and greets, interviews, and sponsored events.

While pro gamers must be capable of practicing several hours a day and learning all about a top competitive game, personality comes into play because, like many athletes, pro gamers are also entertainers. They are sometimes called player-creators because they create streams, videos, and other engaging content for their fans. While streaming, pro gamers interact with fans in the chat. Streamers strive for positive interactions with fans, and their fans feel like they know these celebrities very well because they have spent hours with them during their streams.

Speedrunners are pro gamers who do not concern themselves with points or watching character development scenes. The goal is to finish the game quickly. Speedrunner Mike Uyama has earned $35 million for charity through his Games Done Quick speedrunning events since 2010. Games journalist Petula Dvorak interviewed him during one such event. "It's the wildest thing," Uyama told Dvorak. "It's the fastest $1 million we ever reached. On Wednesday."[28] By the end of the marathon on Sunday, the event earned $3.4 million for charity. Speedrunning shows mastery of a game and demonstrates a player's quickness, agility, and knowledge of the puzzles and enemies that must be overcome.

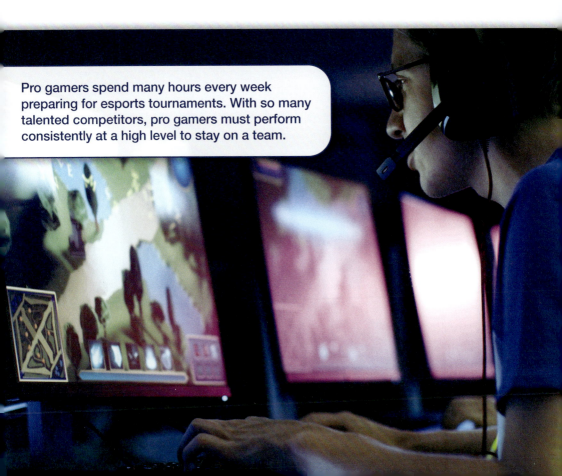

Pro gamers spend many hours every week preparing for esports tournaments. With so many talented competitors, pro gamers must perform consistently at a high level to stay on a team.

Working Conditions

Pro gamers work indoors playing video games while seated in front of monitors, often for eight or more hours a day. Though the best esports organizations strive to strengthen players with physical fitness training, optimal nutrition, coaching, and psychological support, there are hazards. Hand, wrist, and thumb injuries from executing hundreds of actions per minute during gameplay can shorten careers. A thumb injury ended ZooMaa's career at age twenty-five. He explained to disappointed fans that it is "hard for me to compete at the highest level against some of the best players in the world. Playing through the weakness and pain in my hand just isn't possible anymore."[29] Other common physical issues pro gamers face are eyestrain; back, neck, and shoulder pain; and poor sleep. Mental strain from the long hours of practice, incredible pressure of competition, streaming, and online criticism take a toll.

Global travel and meeting top gamers from around the world are big perks. However, travel can be exhausting. Competitions can be exhilarating, but for some players they can cause stage fright and anxiety.

Though competitive gaming is more than a full-time job, these athlete-entertainers also spend time on business opportunities and often stream for several hours at night. Putting in the hours consistently is demanding, but when streamers take a day off, they often lose subscribers. The pro gamer known as DisguisedToast shares, "In this streaming scene, you can't really take breaks. You can't really let up off that gas pedal. You've got to grind, grind, grind, grind, grind."[30]

Employers and Pay

About $4,000 is the average monthly base salary for pro gamers, according to SuperJump video game magazine. If the gamer is part of an esports team, then the organization usually pays for all travel and training expenses, including living expenses while in a game house. In return the organization may keep a percentage

Top Pro Tip: Patience

"[Use patience] inside the game, because there are many moments where it's really tense, like if four people died on each team and it's one on one. If you don't have that patience, you're going to lose that last duel which you wouldn't have otherwise. This can also apply outside of the game. It's going to take you time to get somewhere. . . . I played *League of Legends* for almost two years before I really started improving. I'm sure if I didn't have this patience, I would've given up . . . or I would've allowed myself to not give 110%."

—Martin "Rekkles" Larsson, Swedish pro gamer

Quoted in British Esports Association, "Esports Job Spotlight: Pro Gamer," September 8, 2021. https://britishesports.org.

of the pro gamer's sponsorships, ads, merchandise, and prizes. Currently, there is no union for esports athletes, so players seek assistance from experienced agents to obtain a fair deal.

Since an esports organization may release a player at any time, pro gamers seek other income to stabilize their finances. While most players add thousands of dollars to their income through prizes, sponsorships, and streaming, the top earners add tens of millions of dollars in a year.

What Is the Future Outlook for Pro Gamers?

The global video game industry was expected to grow by 24 percent in 2023, according to a report by the research firm Research and Markets. Industry watchers expect that prize pools will increase in number and amount. The number of teams may grow, creating more slots for professional gamers. Publishers plan to update existing games and launch new games. Meanwhile, manufacturers are developing new technology for hardware, such as gaming gloves, which will create openings for players who are proficient in the new technologies. In an evolving environment, these pros will continue to master the rules of the game in order to win.

Find Out More

Creator Diversity Program from StreamElements
https://Streamelements.com/CreatorDiversity
Creator Diversity is a program to bring diversity into the game industry. Applicants must be streamers, in addition to other requirements. The program includes a twelve-week course, input from a dedicated success manager, and prizes.

Esports Players League
www.espl.co
The league hosts hundreds of mobile-focused esports tournaments and tens of thousands of matches worldwide. Tens of thousands of esports teams compete. Tournaments range from local to global. The site links to its tournament website, team finder, Discord channel, updates, and livestreams.

Women in Games
www.womeningames.org
Women in Games supports gender diversity in the games industry worldwide. Members include esports players and other game industry professionals. The organization presents career and networking events and an annual conference with industry mentors as well as an esports tournament.

SOUND DESIGNER

What Does a Sound Designer Do?

Sound designers infuse video games with rich audio to immerse and instruct players. Completing a level rewards a player with a tune that indicates success. The sound of an enemy character unsheathing a sword elicits a player's instant response. The sounds of a calliope and sideshow barkers bring a virtual circus to life, making players feel like they are within that entertainment world.

Designers create appropriate sounds to match gaming graphics by searching libraries of sound effects. If they cannot find what they want, they record their own.

Sound designers find or create not only sound effects but all the sounds in the game, including background music and voiceovers. They begin work after the game designer defines the story and concept. Then sound designers work closely with game designers, visual artists, and performers to enhance gameplay with real-time sounds that reflect the player's actions and the environment the player navigates. Also, sound designers envelop the entire game in a musical score. Within that

A Few Facts

Pay
Median annual salary of $92,000

Educational Requirements
Bachelor's degree preferred

Personal Qualities
An ear for music, creative, good communication skills

Work Settings
Office or remote

Future Job Outlook
Growth of 21 percent through 2030*

*In all industries, not just video game industry

score, smaller musical pieces, such as character themes, aid player memory and drive player emotion and engagement.

Sound designers use software and hardware to record sound and place audio files in the game. Some sound designers compose and create music or voice characters themselves, especially on smaller projects. On larger projects, sound designers also direct others such as composers, musicians, and voice artists to bring these games to life.

A Typical Workday

The day starts in an office around nine or ten o'clock in the morning with a game team meeting, in which game designers, artists, programmers, and sound designers discuss the progress of the game and give an update on their projects. Even though sound designers work solo at times, sound designer Jaclyn Shumate emphasizes the importance of working well with others on a team. "Communication and collaboration are key, both with any audio colleagues you may have and with the rest of the development team," she says. "This gives the designer an understanding of what audio content needs to be created for the project, and how best to implement audio in the game."[31]

After the meeting, team members are off to their desks, and the sound designers work on projects such as composing music or recording dialogue over background music.

Sometimes, a sound designer may leave the studio for a field recording. For example, a designer may need to record the sound of a person diving into a pool of water or the chatter of a certain type of monkey. At other times, a sound designer might create a specific noise or sound. Aural effects created manually are called Foley sounds. To create sound effects for a treelike character named Ivern in the popular fighting game *League of Legends*, sound designer Bryan Higa says he constructed a Foley prop called the "creaker." He explains, "It's just two pieces of wood, two hinges, and a rope. We wanted Ivern's sound to be distinct.

. . . So we thought creaking would be great, especially for his shield ability. We figured creaking would provide tension and anticipation for players to know when the shield is about to break."[32]

In the afternoon, a designer might work on incorporating music into the game and testing it. As the workday winds down, members of the game team meet for a playthrough of the section of the game they are working on. After discussing what is going well and what needs improvement, most of the team heads home.

Education and Training

According to a 2021 survey by GameSoundCon, a game music and sound design site, 90 percent of recent hires have at least a bachelor's degree. Audio-related degrees in audio engineering, sound design, music, or music production as well as computer science degrees provide good preparation for the field. High school courses in music, computers, and math form a good foundation for a future sound designer.

That Moment I Became Interested in Sound Design

"I was walking down a hallway [in the game *Dead Space*] and just wanted to know why I felt so tense. I started listening more carefully to the music and noticed this ambient violin section that was ascending the whole time and building to a crescendo. I just remember thinking '. . . that's why this game is so scary! It's the sound! I wonder who did that?' I think that's the first time I actually asked myself 'what is a sound designer?'"

—Sergio Ronchetti, sound designer and composer

Quoted in Mat Ombler, "Sergio Ronchetti on How Heavy Metal Inspired His Debut Orchestral Score for *Eldest Souls*," Spitfire Audio, April 14, 2021. https://composer.spitfireaudio.com.

A college degree is usually not required to become a sound designer. Experience, though, is a requirement. Aspiring sound designers gain experience by playing a variety of games, learning how sound enhances a game, and building their library of sound recordings (even on a smartphone). Sound designer David Philipp suggests paying attention to sounds everywhere and always being prepared to record: "Today in the morning I opened my hotel door and it sounded like . . . [MUTO, a monster] of the *Godzilla* movie and yeah so I recorded it and I'll come back to it later and hopefully can use it in one of the future projects."[33]

The process of making a demo reel is good training, and so is replacing the soundscape of a video one knows well. Associate sound designer Alison Ho suggests, "Take something that you find really fun and interesting, and strip the sound out of it, and put some of your own sounds in it. . . . It can really help you grow and learn new things."[34]

Sound designers often enter the field through internships and other introductory jobs at a game studio, such as game tester, runner, or assistant rerecording mixer. Employers also value those who have experience doing DJ work, performing music, or doing audio production.

Skills and Personality

Steve Ouimette, the sound designer behind *Guitar Hero*, describes how his personality led him to develop audio skills at an early age:

> Ever since I was a kid, I used to drive my guitar teachers and the other band members crazy because I couldn't stand when we played a song the wrong way, so I'd sit there with a cassette player or turntable and play back parts until I could figure them out. Then I learned about the karaoke trick of summing the two-track to mono and flipping one channel out of phase so I could hear parts that might be hidden in the mix.[35]

Like Ouimette's desire to investigate how sounds are made and recorded, most sound designers are motivated by curiosity and a desire to solve problems. To create and implement sound, a sound designer will employ a mix of audio and technical skills. Listening skills and an ear for music enable the ability to create and record quality sound. In addition, sound designers use specialized hardware and software to mix, master, and edit audio files and insert them into the game. Along with proficiency with game engines and audio programs, sound designers must be familiar with at least one scripting language, such as Blueprints, C#, Lua, or Python. Employers do not expect prospective sound designers to know all scripting languages, software, and hardware. Studios are looking for people with the ability to learn. The demo reel will show technical fluency. Sound designer Brian Schmidt states, "Being able to create high quality sound and/or music is the primary skill. . . . In the end, it's what comes out of the speakers that counts."[36]

Working Conditions

As with other industry jobs, sound designers work in an office or sound studio; freelancers work from home and may join office meetings or use studio equipment, such as the Foley room. Days are spent in collaboration with teammates, working at computers, and creating sound. Sometimes sound designers go out in the field with their recording equipment to create a sound effect.

Creating a large-budget video game is a monumental task that can require countless hours by hundreds of highly skilled workers and take years to complete. In an effort to get more done more quickly, some employers have a crunch culture. For some employers, regularly working nine- or ten-hour days is not unusual, and to meet deadlines, workers may crunch sixty or more hours a week for weeks on end. "My least favorite part of my job is crunching," shares sound designer Jaclyn Shumate. "Unfortu-

Sound designers infuse video games with rich audio to enhance the feeling of being immersed in the game. The sounds they create match the onscreen action and provide background and voiceovers throughout the game.

nately, long hours are often required to make something sound the way you want it to. Crunch can be part of the career, and can take a toll on your personal life and your health."[37]

Employers and Pay

Video game studios and sound studios hire sound designers. As with artists, sound designers often move between the film and the game industries.

GameSoundCon's 2021 survey reveals a salaried sound designer's median annual income is $92,000. For freelance sound designers and composers, the median income is $30,000 annually. For about 16 percent of freelancers, this amount includes royalties. A royalty is an amount paid to composers, for example, for each time someone plays their music.

Capturing Authentic Animal Noises

"Talk to the people who take care of the animals or who train the animals because they [know] for example before they get fed they're really vocal or if you turn away . . . they start to get vocal. . . . These tricks are really important . . . [to] get the sound you're after. . . . Recordings sometimes can also be dangerous so . . . when recording wildcats or stags in mating season it really is better to be on the other side of the cage or have a very, very long boom pole at your disposal. . . . Just plan your insurance accordingly, I guess."

—David Philipp, sound designer

Quoted in Game Developers Conference, *Next Level Creature Sound Design*, YouTube, January 14, 2021. www.youtube.com/watch?v=Rz7WwwIDjOA.

When a game has a bigger budget, the sound designer may hire musicians or pay to use an existing song. David Perry, president of Shiny Entertainment, explains why a song ended up being the most expensive part of *The Matrix* game *Path of Neo*: "The [writer-directors Lilly and Lana Wachowski]—you've gotta remember, they're cool people who watch a lot of entertainment, and they're kind of fun. . . . They're like, 'we're gonna have "We Are the Champions" playing.' And we're going, 'Do you know how expensive it's gonna be to license that song?' It's like, 'No, no, no. We're gonna have that song.'"[38]

What Is the Future Outlook for Sound Designers?

The Bureau of Labor Statistics forecasts sound designer positions will experience 21 percent growth through 2030 for all industries. Since sound is integral to most video game worlds, sound designers will remain in demand, and their unique contributions will not go unnoticed. Christian Linke, a composer and creative director at Riot Games, asserts, "I think we're living in this golden era where suddenly the world is listening to what videogames have to say."[39]

Find Out More

Game Audio Network Guild
www.audiogang.org

This international organization is for those working in game audio. A scholars program awards both free passes to conferences and mentoring opportunities. The organization's website features *Audio Source Magazine*, annual awards, and a student discount for access to tutorials and other member benefits.

International Game Developers Association (IGDA)
www.igda.org

The IGDA is a nonprofit organization for people who create games. IGDA offers a Discord channel and some programs for students, including: IGDA Scholars awards, discounted student membership, the student portfolio showcase, the student game showcase, and discounts on conferences and game development software.

Overclocked Remix
https://ocremix.org

Overclocked Remix is a nonprofit community for game music professionals and enthusiasts. Its website contains resources for those learning about the field, including interviews with audio professionals and community forums. The site lists links to the game music arrangement community and to albums, bands, performers, labels, and composers.

Sound on Sound
www.soundonsound.com

This site offers podcasts, tutorials, and interviews with audio professionals. There are also forums, *Sound on Sound* magazine, and audio news and information accessible on the site.

GAME TESTER

What Does a Game Tester Do?

Game testers, also called quality assurance (QA) testers, check for errors, or bugs, which affect gameplay and could lead to the game crashing, or stopping in a way that requires restarting to get the game operating again. They also try to "break" the game by performing legal in-game actions that might unbalance or significantly disrupt gameplay, revealing aspects of the game that might need to be limited or recoded to ensure game progress is smooth for players. According to Jason W. Bay, a former tester, "The tester's role is critical because they are the last line of defense before the game is released to players. If they don't do their jobs well, it leads to millions of disappointed fans as they realize the game has bugs, crashes, or—even worse—loses their progress. If you've had that happen, you know how frustrating it is."[40]

Some testers specialize in testing certain aspects of a game. Disability testers may focus on making sure adaptive hardware performs as intended. For example, when a toggle requires too much dexterity or strength, programmers may remap the keyboard so players with disabilities in these areas can use the space bar instead. Localization QA tes-

A Few Facts

Pay
Median annual salary of $55,000

Educational Requirements
High school diploma

Personal Qualities
Observant, analytical, psychomotor skills, good communicator

Work Settings
Office or remote

Future Job Outlook
Estimated rapid growth through 2030

ters work to ensure the language in the game translates accurately. For example, the localization tester ensures a stop sign says "ALTO" when played in its Spanish-language version. Localization testers also make sure a game translates culturally, ensuring that specific holidays, geographical references, and other cultural aspects are included, when possible, to make the game more familiar and immersive for different players around the globe.

A Typical Workday

Catching up on emails starts the day. There may be notifications about a new version of the game or requests from programmers to test a fix. Testers may gather with a quality assurance team for updates and assignments. The goal of the QA team is to make sure the game plays smoothly and without glitches regardless of player skill level.

Back at their workstation, testers plan a systematic approach to test an area of gameplay, looking for bugs and design flaws. Testers may engage a character with every element within a scene to find a bug. Or, as a QA tester known on Reddit forums as u/letsqatest describes, testers try to break the game: "Breaking a game is usually about being creative. You have an objective to click a button and then pick up a ball. This is what players are more apt to do. But what happens if you first pick up the ball and then press the button? If something unintended happens, especially if it breaks progression or causes the game to crash—this is considered breaking the game."[41]

When testers discover a bug or flaw that they can reliably replicate, they write detailed reports identifying what they found, where it occurred in the game, and how they made it happen. These reports help the software developers find the bug and develop a fix.

Education and Training

For someone who is passionate about video games and wishes to work in the game industry, the QA tester position can be a way to enter the field. Entry-level testers may only need a high school diploma to secure a job. Having a college degree in computer science, software engineering, or a related field is attractive to an employer and is more likely to lead to a higher-paying job with more interesting responsibilities.

Testers perform a wide range of activities based on their education and experience. While a beginning tester may find and document bugs, software development testers may write or modify programs that will automatically check for certain types of errors.

High school courses in areas such as coding, computer science, communication, and English (writing) are good preparation. QA testers write a lot of reports, so their communication skills must be good. Aspiring testers can also prepare by creating or modifying their own games.

Some studios hire students as beta testers or interns. This can be a way to get some experience. Beta testers "play test" a version of the game that is almost ready to launch. By this point the game has already been through standard testing and has undergone most fixes. Beta testers are a last check on the game; they play the game all the way through to spot any lingering issues. It can be more fun and less demanding than a typical tester's work but is still an important position. After all, any type of work experience in the game industry provides an opportunity to learn and can lead to future employment.

Skills and Personality

Studios prefer that testers have extensive gaming experience with many different types of games and platforms. Generally, testers have good reaction time, dexterity, and vision. Specialized testers such as software development testers, localization testers, and testers with disabilities may not require these skills to the same extent.

Testers need to understand the logic behind the rules of the game. For example, if a game rule is that a player needs at least 500 points to acquire a special power, the tester will look for

> ### A Great Way to Start
>
> "Starting your career as a QA Tester is one of the best ways to get into the video game industry, and it's a great way to learn about how game studios work and how games are made. I know many people who started as testers and then went on to become producers, artists, designers, or programmers. In fact, I started my career as a tester and later went on to run a large game studio!"
>
> —Jason W. Bay, product manager in ecommerce and video games at Amazon
>
> Jason W. Bay, "All Careers in the Video Game Industry," Game Industry Career Guide, February 9, 2021. www.gameindustrycareerguide.com.

instances when a player can acquire the power with fewer than 500 points.

Game testers also need patience and diligence. In an interview with the online magazine Mental Floss, Jason W. Bay, author of *Land a Job as a Video Game Tester*, states, "Testers spend most of their time testing the game long before it's finished, and long before it starts to become a fun experience. Even after the game is developed enough to start being fun, the testing assignments often aren't fun at all."[42]

Communication skills are key. Testers must be able to explain to others in writing and orally what the problem is and how to recreate it. They also need analysis skills and creativity to figure out how to break games. And since testers often critique the work of team members, tact is a valuable attribute.

Working Conditions

For someone with a passion for gaming, working as a tester can be a dream come true. There are many perks, such as working with other gamers and being able to play games before they are released to the public. Sometimes a tester may even get

Exposing Those Bugs

"You will be simultaneously loved and hated by the development team. Programmers love to despise their QA team and often scream out in rage (good spirited, of course) while the more professional ones learn and realize that it's a particularly excellent QA tester who can expose those nasty bugs and make their code better. The good QA testers rise quickly, sometimes even breaking ground on a career path to design or production. It's widely considered to be a gateway job to those roles and from what I've witnessed, in most companies, it's fairly easy to stand out in QA by being good, professional and communicating well with developers."

—Darryl Wright, president and technical director of video game maker Ubisoft

Darryl Wright, "What Is It like to Be a Video Game Tester?," Quora, 2018. https://www.quora.com.

to meet a famous game creator. Bayaar Lo-Borjiged, a former tester who is now the chief executive officer of Skull Fire Games and a *Metal Gear* fan, told Mental Floss that he was thrilled when Hideo Kojima, creator of *Metal Gear*, came to visit the studio one day. "I was able to meet one of gaming's biggest legends,"[43] says Lo-Borjiged.

Most testers work in an office environment with a team. That is one of the best parts for tester Adrian Hsiah, who says, "You spend most of your time in an environment with other like-minded people, who love video games, usually around your age. There's a camaraderie that develops."[44]

There are potential downsides, though. Testers often have little job stability, sometimes receive low pay, and may be subject to excessive overtime. When a game is nearing release or a deadline, testers may work extra hours. Some testers even report working through the night and sleeping under their desks.

Employers and Pay

Game studios and outside staffing companies are the main employers for game testers. Testers working directly for a studio usually receive better employment terms, such as permanent status, full-time hours, health benefits, and opportunities for advancement. Some may even get their name in the game's credits. When a staffing company hires testers on a temporary basis or as contractors, there may be no benefits or job security.

For a person with no degree and no experience, the first tester position may pay minimum wage. Hours vary from part time to full time, and there can be overtime. If testers are paid a set amount (salary) as opposed to an hourly rate, they may not receive additional pay for overtime. Many testers are employed less than a year at each job because there is a seasonality to game development. Once a game launches, fewer people are needed, and not all get shuffled to other projects. It is a good idea to research the employer to understand the work conditions beforehand.

When a tester has experience and a degree in a related field, the pay and benefits increase. According to ZipRecruiter, which bases estimates on job postings and payroll data, as of 2021, the video game tester salary ranged from about $18,000 a year for an entry-level position to about $106,000 for a seasoned professional with a degree. The median salary for those with a degree and about five years' experience was about $55,000.

What Is the Future Outlook for Game Testers?

The world's nearly insatiable appetite for entertainment exploded during the pandemic since more people were at home. This trend continues, with gaming at the forefront. The demand for entertainment ensures a bright outlook both for the video game industry and for testers. According to the Bureau of Labor Statistics, the number of jobs is expected to grow by about 66 percent by 2030 for the software developers, quality assurance analysts, and testers classification in the motion picture and video industries. Video game testers, though, may only see a small percentage of that growth.

Find Out More

AbleGamers
https://ablegamers.org

This nonprofit advocates for people with disabilities to be able to play video games. Its "Player Panels" project pays people with disabilities to test games and advise the industry on accessibility. AbleGamers also trains and certifies game developers in accessible player experience.

Association for Software Testing (AST)
https://associationforsoftwaretesting.org

The AST blog, Slack channel, and annual conference provide ways to learn more about the QA testing profession. In addition, AST's Twitter feed shares events and information for testers.

International Game Developers Association (IGDA)
www.igda.org

This nonprofit membership organization offers some programs for students, such as the IGDA Scholars award for college students and discounted student membership. Resources such as the student portfolio showcase, the student game showcase, and discounts on conferences and game development software are available to members.

SOURCE NOTES

Introduction: Working in the Business of Play

1. Quoted in Ted Price, "Marvel's Guardians of the Galaxy with Jean-François Dugas and Mary DeMarle," AIAS Game Maker's Notebook, January 25, 2022. https://interactive.libsyn.com.
2. Quoted in Tom Regan, "What Goes On at an Esports Bootcamp? Go Behind the Scenes with Rix.GG. . . ," Red Bull, December 8, 2021. www.redbull.com.
3. Quoted in Ryan Pearson, "Activision Blizzard Not Part of the Game Awards 2021 Beyond Nominations, Confirms Geoff Keighley," Bounding into Comics, December 6, 2021. https://boundingintocomics.com.
4. Amalie Kae, *Writing for Video Games: Why It's Different from Other Industries*, YouTube, August 1, 2020. www.youtube.com/watch?v=GXUrWtGZH3s.

Game Artist

5. Quoted in Tim Colwill, "Game Developers Need to Unionize: A Union Can Work in This Business, and Other Industries Have Proven It," Polygon, January 16, 2019. www.polygon.com.
6. Quoted in Riot Games, *So You Wanna Make Games?? Episode 2: Concept Art*, YouTube, December 13, 2018. www.youtube.com/watch?v=FqX-UMVTLHI.
7. Quoted in Riot Games, *So You Wanna Make Games?? Episode 2*.
8. Quoted in Jason W. Bay, "How to Become a Video Game Concept Artist," Game Industry Career Guide, 2021. www.gameindustrycareerguide.com.
9. Quoted in Jason W. Bay, "How to Become a Video Game Special Effects Artist," Game Industry Career Guide, September 7, 2021. www.gameindustrycareerguide.com.
10. Quoted in Riot Games, *So You Wanna Make Games?? Episode 2*.
11. Quoted in Jason W. Bay, "What Does It Take to Succeed as a 2D Artist/Animator in Video Games?," Game Industry Career Guide, 2021. www.gameindustrycareerguide.com.
12. Quoted in Alex Kane, "An Oral History of *The Matrix* Video Games and Their Bonkers Alternate Ending," Polygon, December 26, 2021. www.polygon.com.

Game Designer

13. Quoted in Teddy Amenabar, "'Elder Scrolls Online' Creative Director Says 'New World' Popularity Will 'Shake Things Up,'" *Washington Post*, October 4, 2021. www.washingtonpost.com.
14. Quoted in Rachel Koo, "Reflections as a Designer," Rachel Koo's personal website, April 8, 2020. https://rkoo283.wixsite.com.
15. Quoted in Diane Guillemont, "I Am the Game Designer for the Official Mobile Version of *Dead by Daylight*. Ask Me Anything!," Reddit, July 5, 2019. www.reddit.com.
16. Chris Muriel, *What Does a Game Designer Do on a Daily Basis in the AAA Industry?*, Game Design with Chris, YouTube, August 31, 2020. www.youtube.com/watch?v=FjcP9OJRfEE.
17. Quoted in Nemin, "Interview with David Fried," Oddwords, February 6, 2020. https://oddwords.hu.
18. Quoted in Shannon Liao, "A Year into the Pandemic, Game Developers Reflect on Burnout, Mental Health and Avoiding Crunch," *Washington Post*, April 15, 2021. www.washingtonpost.com.
19. Tom Sloper, "Lesson #14: All About the Job of 'Game Designer,'" Sloperama Productions, June 6, 2018. www.sloperama.com.

Game Programmer

20. Quoted in Chris Kerr, "Float On: The Zero-Gravity Physics of Cosmic Puzzler *Heavenly Bodies*," Game Developer, December 8, 2021. www.gamedeveloper.com.
21. Quoted in Jason W. Bay, "How to Become a Video Game Tools Programmer," Game Industry Career Guide, 2021. www.gameindustrycareerguide.com.
22. Quoted in Alicia Haddick, "The Game Developers Who Enable Speedrunners to Break Their Games," Kotaku, December 8, 2021. https://kotaku.com.
23. Quoted in Stephen Gossett, "Want to Be a Game Developer? Here's How," Built In, May 26, 2021. https://builtin.com.
24. Quoted in Gossett, "Want to Be a Game Developer?"
25. Quoted in Gossett, "Want to Be a Game Developer?"

Pro Gamer

26. Quoted in Reece Hiland and David Campbell, "A Day in the Life of an Esports Gamer," MPN, August 10, 2021. www.mpn.ca.
27. Quoted in Intel, "The Daily Regimen of Players in Professional Gaming," June 17, 2021. www.intel.com.
28. Quoted in Petula Dvorak, "His Mom Didn't Nag When He Was a Lost 20-Something Playing Video Games in Her Basement. $35

Million Later, She's Glad She Didn't," *Washington Post*, January 13, 2022. www.washingtonpost.com.
29. ZooMaa, "Taking a Step Back from Competitive *Call of Duty*. . . ," Twit Longer, January 19, 2020. www.twitlonger.com.
30. Quoted in Nathan Grayson, "Top Streamers Are Leaving Twitch Amidst Big Money and Shady Deals," Kotaku, January 30, 2020. https://kotaku.com.

Sound Designer

31. Quoted in Jason W. Bay, "How to Become a Video Game Sound Designer," Game Industry Career Guide, 2021. www.gameindustrycareerguide.com.
32. Quoted in Riot Games, *So You Wanna Make Games?? Episode 8: Sound Design*, YouTube, December 13, 2018. www.youtube.com/watch?v=KcorIwJscFA.
33. David Philipp, *Next Level Creature Sound Design*, Game Developers Conference, YouTube, January 14, 2021. www.youtube.com/watch?v=Rz7WwwlDjOA.
34. Quoted in Riot Games, *So You Wanna Make Games?? Episode 8*.
35. Quoted in Sam Inglis, "Steve Ouimette: Re-recording Hits for Video Games," *Sound on Sound*, July 2020. www.soundonsound.com.
36. Brian Schmidt, "Game Audio Job Skills—How to Get Hired as a Game Sound Designer," GameSoundCon, September 3, 2020. www.gamesoundcon.com.
37. Quoted in Bay, "How to Become a Video Game Sound Designer."
38. Quoted in Kane, "An Oral History of *The Matrix* Video Games and Their Bonkers Alternate Ending."
39. Quoted in League of Legends, *Dev Diary: The Music of Arcane*, YouTube, November 24, 2021. www.youtube.com/watch?v=cMzi3-2Nct0.

Game Tester

40. Jason W. Bay, "All Careers in the Video Game Industry," Game Industry Career Guide, February 9, 2021. www.gameindustrycareerguide.com.
41. Quoted in Darklife, "Interview with QA Tester—Is Playing Video Games for Money as Easy as Advertised?," Mulehorn Gaming, March 27, 2019. https://mulehorngaming.com.
42. Quoted in Suzanne Raga, "12 Secrets of Video Game Testers," Mental Floss, June 23, 2017. www.mentalfloss.com.
43. Quoted in Raga, "12 Secrets of Video Game Testers."
44. Adrian Hsiah, "Is Game Testing Fun?," Quora, 2022. www.quora.com.

INTERVIEW WITH A GAME DESIGNER

David "Designer Dave" Fried is a game and narrative designer currently living in Thailand. He has more than twenty-three years of game industry experience. He answered questions about his career by email.

Q: Why did you become a game designer?

A: I became a game designer almost by chance. I originally wanted to be a writer and was attending college to obtain an English degree. However, I was running out of money. . . . So I called Blizzard Entertainment in Irvine where I was going to college. I asked if they had any need for people experienced with Macintosh computers, and they actually did because Diablo and *StarCraft* Macintosh versions were being worked on. So, I applied for a Quality Assurance job and got it. From there I took an interest in using their map editor, Star edit, to help ease testing. From that I learned a lot about their trigger system and was able to start making custom maps. So, when they asked for submissions for the *StarCraft* Map of the Month program, I had something to show. I also made a campaign map for the N64 version of *StarCraft* and wrote the story for it and moved into a Level Design position. From there I worked on *Warcraft III: The Frozen Throne*, and then because of my background in writing, I became a Quest designer for *World of Warcraft*. . . . It all started with a random phone call to a game company that just happened to be in the area.

Q: Can you describe your typical workday?

A: There's really no such thing as a typical workday for me anymore. . . . When I worked at major studios, it was a pretty bog standard job. You drive into work in the morning, and you start working on a level for a game or a story idea for a quest. Sometimes that would involve a 3D program like Maya, or it might be a proprietary tool like War Edit for *Warcraft III*. Most of my day would be spent in some form of creative process, and if there were deadlines, there'd often be late hours.

These days it's much more hectic. I might be meeting with clients to advise them on their game or writing lore for a new game studio's first game. I'm currently working on 6 different game projects.

Q: What do you like most about your job?
A: Right now, what I love most about it is the creative freedom. I'm at a point in my career where I can just tell people, "No, I don't want to work on that." That's something that you can't really do early on in a game design career unless you're a full-stack indie developer (that is, a developer that controls an entire game system or application). It's one of the trade-offs of working for yourself and becoming very well rounded and able to do almost every part of game development, versus being extremely specialized in a few areas.

Q: What do you like least about your job?
A: Corporate entities. They really are the worst and whenever I work with them there's always restrictive brick walls that prevent creative freedom. There's a Demotivator poster that sums it up quite succinctly. "Meetings: None of us is as dumb as all of us." I find that when there's too many layers of input, all the intrigue and life can be drained from the creative process until it becomes tepid and mediocre. Risk averse corporate entities will always push you towards the known and avoid the unfamiliar. . . . I thrive on the unfamiliar because that's where growth is.

Q: What personal qualities do you find most valuable for this type of work?
A: Every designer is different and can have their own areas of expertise. Those with a mathematical inclination can become amazing systems and mechanics designers. Those with a creative flair

can be great narrative and level designers. People with a love for action can become combat designers. There's really a design discipline for everyone, which is why no two designers that you'll ever meet will ever think alike on every topic. It's that diversity that makes the work so interesting, because two people can approach the same problem and come up with wildly different but functional ideas. The real question is: Can you commit to one vision, and which concept suits the vision best? That's often what separates good designers from great ones, the ability to set aside personal preference to match a vision that may not be their own.

Q: What advice do you have for students who are interested in this career?

A: The most important advice for any aspiring game designer is to recognize your areas of knowledge and acknowledge your areas of ignorance. No one is perfect, no one knows everything. So, pretending you know something when you don't denies you the opportunity to learn more about it. I've been making games for 23 years, but there are always new areas that I run into where I can't be certain of the best approach, or there might be new techniques I'm not experienced with. Recognizing that lack of experience allows me to accept that I still have more to learn and thus become a better designer. All of life is a learning process that is the fabled "journey" that matters more than the destination. It's the path you choose to take when designing something that matters more than the end result, whether it be a success or failure. If you learned something new, you're now a better designer for it, and that's the best outcome you can hope for.

OTHER JOBS IN THE GAMING INDUSTRY

Art director
Brand manager
Community coordinator
Curator for electronic games museum
Data scientist—artificial intelligence
Esports broadcast producer
Esports product manager
Esports trainer
Foreign language translator
Game director
Games journalist
Influencer marketing specialist
Insights analyst
Legal counsel (attorney)
Live broadcast producer
Market analyst
Marketing manager
Motion capture director
Partner marketing
Pipeline engineer
Player support agent
Producer
Product manager
Pro gamer agent
Public relations manager/publicist
Retail game store associate
Session musician
Social media strategist
Sound engineering technician
Stunt actor
Technical support specialist
User research moderator
Video game industry recruiter
Video manager
Virtual event host
Web developer

Editor's note: The online *Occupational Outlook Handbook* of the US Department of Labor's Bureau of Labor Statistics is an excellent source of information on jobs in hundreds of career fields, including many of those listed here. The *Occupational Outlook Handbook* may be accessed online at www.bls.gov/ooh.

INDEX

Note: Boldface page numbers indicate illustrations.

AbleGamers, 52
Academy of Interactive Arts & Sciences (AIAS), 21
Academy of Interactive Arts & Sciences Foundation (AIAS), 13
AIGA, 21
Association for Software Testing (AST), 52

Bahtijaragic, Elvir, 24
Bay, Jason W., 46, 49
Bureau of Labor Statistics (BLS), 59
   on game artist, 13
   on game programmer, 28
   on game tester, 51–52
   on sound designer, 44

Creator Diversity Program (StreamElements), 37
crunch (working long hours), 5, 12, 27

DeMarle, Mary, 4
Develteam (website), 29
Dvorak, Petula, 34

Esports Players League, 37

Finney, Tyler, 10
Foley sounds, 39
Fried, David "Designer Dave," 19, 56–58

game artist, **10**
   educational requirements, 7, 8–9
   employers of, 12
   future job outlook, 7, 13
   information resources, 13–14
   number of jobs, 7
   role of, 7–8
   salary/earnings, 7, 12–13
   skills/personal qualities, 7, 9–10
   typical workday, 8
   working conditions, 11–12
   work settings, 7
Game Audio Network Guild, 45
game designer
   educational requirements, 15, 17–18
   employers of, 19–20
   future job outlook, 15, 20–21
   information resources, 21
   interview with, 56–58
   number of jobs, 15
   role of, 15–16
   salary/earnings, 15, 19–20
   skills/personal qualities, 15, 18
   typical workday, 16–17
   working conditions, 19
   work settings, 15
Game Developer (website), 29
Game Developers Association (IGDA), 5
GameDev.net, 29
game programmer, **26**
   educational requirements, 22, 25–26

employers of, 28
future job outlook, 22
information resources, 29
role of, 22–24
salary/earnings, 22, 28
skills/personal qualities, 22, 26–27
typical workday, 24–25
working conditions, 27–28
work settings, 22
game tester
educational requirements, 46, 47–48
employers of, 51
future job outlook, 46, 51–52
information resources, 52
role of, 46–47
salary/earnings, 46, 51
skills/personal qualities, 46, 48–49
typical workday, 47
working conditions, 49–50
work settings, 46
gaming industry
challenges of careers in, 5–6
other jobs in, 59
gender discrimination/harassment, 5–6
Gish, Brian, 23, 27
Graczyk, Matt, 23–24

Hart, Ryan "Prodigal Son," 33
Higa, Bryan, 39–40
Ho, Alison, 41
Hsiah, Adrian, 50
Hubbell, Nathaniel, 9, 10–11

International Game Developers Association (IGDA), 5, 21, 29, 45, 52

Kabbani, Ali "Myth," 31

Kae, Amalie, 6
Kaplan, Steve, 8
Keighley, Geoff, 6
Kojima, Hideo, 50

Lambert, Richard, 16
Larsson, Martin "Rekkles," 36
Linke, Christian, 44–45
Lo-Borjiged, Bayaar, 50
Loose, Joseph "Luzuh," 5
Low, Pete, 16–17

Muriel, Chris, 17, 18

Occupational Outlook Handbook (Bureau of Labor Statistics), 59
opinion polls. *See* surveys
Ouimette, Steve, 41
Overclocked Remix, 45

Perrin, Alexander, 22–23
Perry, David, 44
Persson, Markus "Notch," 28
Philipp, David, 41, 44
polls. *See* surveys
pro gamer, **34**
educational requirements, 30, 32
employers of, 35–36
future job outlook, 36–37
global esports growth, 30
information resources, 37
number of jobs, 30
role of, 30–31
salary/earnings, 30, 35–36
skills/personal qualities, 30, 33–34
typical workday, 31–32
working conditions, 35
work settings, 30

quality assurance (QA) tester. *See* game tester

Real-Time VFX (website), 13–14
Recruiter.com, 20
Research and Markets, 36
Ronchetti, Sergio, 40

Salary.com, 12, 20
Schmidt, Brian, 42
Shumate, Jaclyn, 39, 42–43
Smith, Keagen "P3NGU1N," 31
software development engineers in test (SDETs), 23
sound designer, **43**
   educational requirements, 38, 40–41
   employers of, 43–44
   future job outlook, 38, 44–45
   information resources, 45
   role of, 38–39
   salary/earnings, 38, 43–44
   skills/personal qualities, 38, 41–42
   typical workday, 39–40
   working conditions, 42–43
   work settings, 38

Sound on Sound, 45
So You Wanna Make Games?? (Riot Games), 14
speedrunners, 23–24, 34
Strom, Allie, 8
Sun, Cody, 32
surveys
   on educational levels in sound design, 40
   on long hours/job insecurity in gaming industry, 5
   on median income in sound design, 43

Uyama, Mike, 34

van der Schyf, Willem, 11

Wardle, 20
Wardle, Josh, 20
Warnock, Shawn, 24–25
Werner, Rich, 11, 12
Whitehall, Gino, 9
Women in Games, 37
Wright, Darryl, 50

ZipRecruiter, 51

PICTURE CREDITS

Cover: RyanKing999/iStock

10: Frame Stock Footage/Shutterstock.com

26: BalanceFormCreative/Shutterstock.com

34: Gorodenkoff/Shutterstock.com

43: Nejron Photo/Shutterstock.com

ABOUT THE AUTHOR

Celia McCarty is a writer and editor in technical and educational fields. She worked with teens and young adults as a social worker and para educator.